RJ

860130

Jin
Otter

THE
GEORGIAN CITIES
OF BRITAIN

Opposite: *Bath. Pulteney Bridge, 1769–74. Robert Adam.*

THE
GEORGIAN CITIES
OF BRITAIN

Kerry Downes

Phaidon · Oxford

Opposite: *Bury St Edmunds. Market Hall (now Town Hall), 1775–8. Robert Adam.*

The author and publishers would like to acknowledge individuals and institutions who have supplied illustrations: Aerofilms Ltd pp. 11, 27, 52. Architectural Association p. 20. J. Bethell pp. 6, 35. Cooper-Bridgeman Library pp. 15, 38–9, 64. City of Liverpool/Stewart Bale Ltd p. 30. Eagle Photos p. 54. Mary Evans Picture Library p. 18. Fotique, Bath p. 33. Ivan Hall p. 46. Angelo Hornak pp. 17, 25, 44–5, 56–7. A. F. Kersting pp. 7, 9, 14, 23, 32, 42, 59. Mansell Collection pp. 41, 50–1. Pix Photos, jacket, title page. J. Rendel Ridges p. 10. John Rowan p. 40. Crown copyright: Royal Commission on Historical Monuments, England pp. 5, 8, 28, 31, 36, 47, 58, 60, 62. Crown copyright: Royal Commission on Ancient Monuments, Scotland pp. 12, 48. Crown copyright: Victoria and Albert Museum p. 24 (J. Malton, 1800). Victoria Art Gallery, Bath City Council pp. 26, 29. Reece Winstone p. 53. Picture research by Linda Proud. Design by Adrian Hodgkins.

Phaidon Press Limited
Littlegate House, St Ebbe's Street, Oxford

First published 1979
© Phaidon Press Limited

Printed in Great Britain by
Hazell Watson & Viney Ltd
Aylesbury, Bucks

Ideas of the Georgian City

'No Nation under Heaven', wrote the portrait painter Jonathan Richardson in 1715, 'so nearly resembles the ancient Greeks and Romans as we. There is a Haughty Courage, an Elevation of Thought, a Greatness of Taste, a Love of Liberty, a Simplicity, and Honesty amongst us, which we inherit from our Ancestors, and which belong to us as Englishmen; and 'tis in These the Resemblance consists.'

Thus at the outset of the Georgian era were the virtues of Athenian democracy and Republican Rome discerned in Georgian Britain by a contemporary of the first of the Georges, one of the generation whose youth saw the personal reign of Charles II (1660–1685), whose twenties saw the 'Glorious' (because bloodless) revolution of 1688 and in whose middle age, in 1714, a Hanoverian monarch succeeded to the English throne.

A little over a century later, in June 1826, the Quarterly Review recalled to its classically educated readers Suetonius's words about the first of the Caesars:

> *Augustus at Rome was for building renown'd,*
> *And of marble he left what of brick he had found;*
> *But is not our Nash, too, a very great master?*
> *He finds us all brick, and he leaves us all plaster.*

Augustus was the first, and the least imperial, of the Roman Emperors, and it was the literature, not the political successes of his age which caused his name to be given to the Early Georgian period. Nevertheless the imperial flavour of John Nash's London was apparent.

The stuccoed façades and colonnades of Nash's Regent Street and

Bath. The Circus, begun 1754. John Wood the Elder.

Regent's Park, conceived in 1811, were mediocre as architecture but unsurpassed as man-made scenery. Nash's control, and his interest, lay not in the details which characterize a great architect but in the overall effect, designed to be seen briefly, broadly, and perhaps kinetically at the speed of a horse-drawn carriage. The imperial allusion was obvious in the scale of his terraces (three and a half miles of them) and the manipulation of early planning procedures towards the desired monumental end. Yet between the architecture of real emperors and Nash's London there was a deep irony: the joint forces behind Nash's scenery were the taste of a constitutional monarch and the relentless urge of the speculative builder to recover his capital outlay with interest. Beneath the high ideal of the Georgian City there lay a reality that was hard-headed, sometimes sordid, and almost always concerned with money.

In 1801 over three-quarters of the population of Great Britain lived in the country; although the proportion of town dwellers was rising fast, Britain even in 1830 was largely rural. But the Industrial Revolution depended not only on advances in the making of iron and the design of machinery but also on a steadily increasing population. The new processes of manufacture did not dispense with human labour but rather depended for larger output on concentrating labour in large teams: one cloth mill replaced many separate weavers' houses; a power loom produced more cloth more quickly than a hand loom. Industrial suburbs grew up, and with them the division between pleasant towns and unpleasant industrial ones; in London, Manchester, Leeds, Birmingham and other cities the prevailing wind was beginning to make the western suburbs the desirable ones.

Cities were also growing closer together with better roads and lighter vehicles; in 1800 Bath was only a day from London by stage coach. York was thirty-one hours; both journey times had been cut by more than half in a century. At a slower pace, an eighty-seat canal boat plied between Manchester and Warrington in 1772 and later between Manchester and Runcorn, although it was to the transport of freight and building materials that the late Georgian canals contributed most. Early in Victorian times the growth of the railways would, through a new combination of speed, smoothness and reliability in travel, cause far more people to travel more widely and often, and holidays would no longer be restricted to the wealthy and their servants. Even in country districts railway time would become the touchstone. But if Georgian Britain did not yet live by

Cheltenham. Promenade, c.1823.

[7]

Manchester. Old Town Hall, King Street (destroyed), 1822–5. Francis Goodwin.

the clock, Georgian cities did not live entirely by the sun either; one of the basic conventions of city life is that only peasants and cattle go to bed at nightfall.

Since the late thirteenth century London had been the undisputed mercantile and political capital of England, setting the standards by which all other places were provincial. After the Act of Union of 1707 Edinburgh retained a measure of capital status in Scotland through the autonomy of the Scottish church and legal system and, not least, through Scottish self-esteem. Scottish enterprise in the eighteenth century was divided between those who wanted to make Edinburgh the modern Rome or Athens and those who moved south with the aim of outdoing the English on their own ground — in architecture notably Colen Campbell, the prophet of Palladianism, and Robert Adam and his brothers. The 'drift to the South' so frequently discussed by modern planners and sociologists was well established in the seventeenth century; successive rulers from Elizabeth I to Oliver Cromwell tried to limit new building in and around London because the supply of food and the road system could not cater for a growth in urban population. The Great Fire of

Edinburgh. Register House, 1774–92. Robert Adam. The national document repository for Scotland was an integral part of the first Edinburgh New Town scheme, 1766.

London in 1666 caused new building standards to be established which ultimately gave the Georgian city its character: it also ended the policy of restriction and thus ensured the primacy of London.

Yet not all roads led to London: Defoe in the 1720s described a 'cross-post' set up by the Post-Master General between the southwest and the Humber, connecting ports and cloth towns. From Plymouth it ran through Exeter, Taunton, Bridgwater, Bristol, Gloucester, Worcester, Bridgnorth, Chester, Liverpool, Warrington, Manchester, Bury, Rochdale, Halifax, Leeds and York to Hull. York especially, with the second archbishopric in the land, might claim to be another metropolis, and in 1752 a northern visitor to London found Wren's St Paul's 'a very Grand building, yet I think . . . not quite so uniform as the minster at York'. Besides building themselves town houses the Georgian owners of huge Yorkshire farming and forestry estates commissioned public buildings in York. From the 1720s and 30s survive the Mansion House, Judge's Lodging and Assembly Rooms, from the 1770s the Women's Prison, Assize Courts and County Lunatic Asylum, from the 1820s the Grecian home of the Philosophical Society.

York. Assembly Rooms, 1730–2. Richard Boyle, 3rd Earl of Burlington. One of the most consciously 'Roman' interiors of the Georgian period.

What distinguishes Georgian York, however, is the combination of its Roman past, its size, its access (which we now forget) as a port to French and Portuguese wines, Norwegian timber, and coal by sea and river, and its 'confluence of the gentry' and 'persons of distinction'. The eighteenth century opened with the third Earl of Carlisle's commission to his kinsman John Vanbrugh, still unknown as an architect, for a palace fifteen miles north of the city. Lord Carlisle had chosen to retire from career politics in London to develop his Yorkshire estates as a moral duty, and the scale of Castle Howard, with its domed entrance hall and predominance of state rooms over living quarters, gave a new meaning to the term *great house*. In politics the Whigs had established the Hanoverian Protestant succession and the constitutional character of British monarchy; in architecture they appropriated to their own houses the scale and the lavishness of decoration that had been proper to the Stuart absolutist kings. Castle Howard, which Horace Walpole, unprepared, found 'at one view a palace, a town, a fortified city', stood in relation to York like a Hampton Court or a Versailles to its capital.

In the first quarter of the eighteenth century Vanbrugh himself was a frequent visitor at Castle Howard and at the York assemblies; there he discreetly courted and won his Yorkshire bride, and he recorded a week he spent there in August 1721: 'A Race every day, and a Ball every night; with as much well look'd Company as ever I saw got together The Ladies I mean in Chief.' For an observer as shrewd and serious as Vanbrugh, York's significance was social, even frivolous. It was also local: York imported and consumed, and had no other trade. It had the virtues and the defects of remoteness from London, but during the second quarter of the eighteenth century its status as the focus of elegant provincial society began to pass to Bath. In about 1770 the travellers in Smollett's *Humphry Clinker* spent only a day at York, to see the Minster, the Prison and the Assembly Rooms. By that time, as they soon discovered, Edinburgh had become the social and cultural capital of the North. In 1812 Madame de Staël's declared intention in visiting Britain

Edinburgh. Charlotte Square from the air, looking north. Beyond, from left to right, are Ainslie Place, Moray Place and the beginning of Royal Circus.

Edinburgh. Moray Place, c.1822–30. This hexagonal place is part of the New Town developed for the Earl of Moray by James Gillespie Graham.

was to pass a winter in Edinburgh 'in order to breathe that learned and philosophical air'.

Both for its intellectual life and for its architecture Edinburgh must be considered the most important late Georgian city after London and Bath. But the growth and diversification of Britain's foreign trade, and the mechanical innovations which made her the leader of the world in the Industrial Revolution, produced a new kind of town with a new kind of society. The first wet dock at Liverpool was begun in 1709; by 1800 on average fourteen ships every day of the year passed through the port. While at that date the homes of most of Liverpool's 75,000 inhabitants were undistinguished, civic pride was manifest in a magnificent town hall — already once gutted by fire and restored — and other public buildings. The Act of Union of 1707, which gave Scotland equal trade with England and the Colonies, gave a new commercial life to the ancient city of Glasgow through the importing of tobacco, rum and sugar to Newark (Port Glasgow) and other nearby west coast harbours. Coalmining and the smelting, finishing and utilization of metals brought large working populations to South Lancashire, West Yorkshire and the Midlands. Pre-Georgian Birmingham was a small market town, but it had become famous for brassware by 1758, when it seemed to a visitor there 'as if God had created man only for making buttons'. Much of the domestic building in growing industrial towns was no more than decent, some of it even by the standards of the time was less than decent. While improvements in town sanitation during the eighteenth century helped noticeably to prolong life there were no sewers in Glasgow in 1790, and in 1815 there were only forty for a population of 100,000. Statistics such as these may be of more concern to students of social history than to admirers of architecture, but they relate to large urban communities in Georgian Britain. Whether they are stone-built and fronted by giant columns or plainly built of brick, Georgian terrace houses are, as Reyner Banham once observed, a way of stacking people.

The City Ideal

In Britain a city has a cathedral, a royal palace or a charter granted by the Crown. Manchester became a city only in 1853, Liverpool in 1880, Birmingham in 1889. In the United States of America a city need, strictly speaking, be no more than a community governed by a mayor and aldermen, and the word was more loosely used in the newer states of the West. Much of America was settled by men who accepted neither bishops nor kings but looked to the language of the English Bible and of writers who depended upon it – travellers in Bunyan's *Pilgrim's Progress* come to cities. Their towns were often located where travellers grew tired or were caught by nightfall; in Britain this process of settlement had been accomplished so much earlier – more than a thousand years before – that few traces of it remain. Most British towns are at heart overgrown villages or collections of villages. In states like Virginia one can see today from the air towns which were laid out on regular geometrical grid or 'checkerboard' plans, of a kind recommended by Renaissance theorists but rarely feasible at home in an old and widespread civilization.

But while these New World towns were staked out according to a deliberate and regular aesthetic ideal, the settlers enclosed their farms on quite different principles, which they also brought with them, parcelling out small irregular fields according to their use and location. Ancient Roman soldiers had set out their British garrisons on grid plans, but what survived in Britain by the seventeenth century was the pattern of medieval villages which had grown up after the dispersal of Romano-British civilization, through successive waves of new settlers from across the North Sea. In these communities boundaries and thoroughfares followed the lie of the land and natural features like woods and watercourses, and this practice became so ingrained in the British mind that habit can no longer be distinguished from taste. It accounts, as much as any other factor, for the felicity of John Wood's layout in Bath.

Villages grow where there are river crossings, opportunities for trade or manufacture, natural resources, religious houses or seats of secular power. Prosperous villages grew into towns, and Greater

Wisbech. North Brink. Individual Georgian merchants' houses beside the navigable river that runs through the town.

London. Regent Street, looking north from Piccadilly Circus.

London is still an aggregation of villages around the old mercantile capital, the City of London, and the seat of government, the City of Westminster. In the West End of London, parts of Georgian St Marylebone were laid out as new, regular grid suburbs, but Marylebone Lane still meanders through them, following an old stream which has long since been enclosed in a conduit. London as a whole cannot be called a Georgian city, nor even as wholes can Edinburgh or Bath; on the other hand Georgian London, Georgian Edinburgh and Georgian Bath are concepts that can be entertained, supported and illustrated. So too can Georgian Brighton, Cheltenham, Bristol, and, less familiarly, Liverpool, Newcastle, Exeter, Hull, Glasgow, Whitehaven, and others.

These concepts are bound to be nebulous, for several reasons. First of all, while Whitehaven was one of the very few totally new British towns of the eighteenth century, the others grew by degrees from older centres, with less overall control or foresight than tidy-minded modern planners would wish to allow. Moreover the Georgian idea of British liberty excluded at the outset the kind of plan, imposed from above by an almighty sovereign, which had produced the Rome of Renaissance and Baroque Popes, the Versailles

– town and palace – of Louis XIV and Louis XV, the Nancy of Stanislas Leszczynski, or any truly imperial city. Even towards the end of the Georgian period Nash's 'imperial' scheme could be at once admired and parodied, for it consisted of two parts, one of which, Regent Street, bordered on and coordinated several already existing urban developments while the other, Regent's Park, was urban in neither intention nor form. Then also Regent's Park can be considered as the extreme case of a *sub*-urban tendency that, as we shall see, is characteristic of most of Georgian London. Finally, Georgian town building was nearly all speculative, based on the fluctuations of the property market, the financial acumen of developers, the hazards of fashion, and the alternation of peace and war; in both design and execution it was almost always spasmodic.

The constitutional distinction between town and city has already been disregarded in this discussion; in French the primary sense of *cité* is the totality of inhabitants, *ville* (town) is the sum of buildings. In Britain the ideal underlying both terms is less a physical than a social one. Twentieth-century planners are still slow to learn that bricks and mortar and concrete, even benches and flowerbeds, do not make a community. Georgian Bath was as much the sum – or something greater than the sum – of its inhabitants as of its structures. Indeed it was the political and social ideas of eighteenth-century Britain that made Georgian Bath possible.

The ultimate social model was the city-state of Ancient Athens: T. H. Shepherd's illustrations of Edinburgh (1829) were entitled *Modern Athens*. The educated Georgian citizen's knowledge of Athens was mainly literary, through the Greek and Roman classics, but those who had finished their education by making the Grand Tour to Italy knew something also of a more modern but still historic republic: Venice, which has for centuries enamoured the British, like most other Northern travellers. The Greek *polis* (city) gave us the words *politics* (the balance of power) and *police* (its orderly maintenance) just as the Latin *civitas* gave us *city*, *citizen*, *civic*, *civilization*. Other words, however, had in the eighteenth century rather different connotations from their modern ones: *republic* (Latin, *affairs of the people*) and *democracy* (Greek, *rule of the people*) depended on quite a different understanding of *the people*.

London. Bedford Square, 1775–80. Attributed to Thomas Leverton.

The Athenian democracy had been governed by an assembly in which all citizens were represented. If it worked as well, as fairly and as intelligently as we are led to believe, that was for two reasons. First, the population was small, and second, by no means all inhabitants were citizens. The large class of slaves, who were the property of their masters, had restricted rights; though some acquired education, they had no vote. The Roman Republic carried on this system; the unprivileged found it on the whole acceptable – knowing no other – and the freemen found it admirable. But Rome grew too large, too populous and eventually too widespread and imperial to do without an emperor. The spread of Christianity, especially after the Emperor Constantine was converted early in the fourth century AD, gave a new authority and sanctity to the paternal

Dublin. The Four Courts, 1786–1802. James Gandon.

system which was the basis of many European tribes, since both the Old and New Testaments abound in references to kingship, whether of Christ or of David and the patriarchs. By the seventeenth century the crowned and anointed heads of Europe saw themselves as fathers of their people like Abraham and as kings like David, dispensing wisdom and justice like Solomon by divine authority.

Not everyone, however, agreed with them: there were magnates who wished to convert their wealth into political power, philosophers who valued the state above the ruler, secular idealists who wished to return to a republican system, and religious idealists who saw all men as equal before God and would therefore have no hierarchy in between, whether of bishops or princes. Of such men was made the English Parliament which convinced itself in 1648–9 that the king had sinned against the state. In the troubled years that followed the execution of Charles I for high treason, there were some who wished to set up a popular republic in which every man had a vote, but the scheme came to an abrupt end when it was realized that, numerically, the poor would therefore rule the middle class. The first step in the great British compromise was the restoration of the monarchy in 1660, and although a cynic might say it was for want of anything better, one gauge of the enduring value of the British monarchy is the acclaim it receives today in countries, especially France and the United States, which have none of their own.

A further step was taken in 1688. James II was trying to rule without Parliament and to restore England to Roman Catholicism. In the ensuing crisis James was permitted to escape with his life and Parliament, in the name of the 'people', offered the throne to Prince William of Orange and Mary Stuart who were, respectively, his nephew and son-in-law and his eldest daughter.

The Golden Age and its Limitations

Thus the Glorious Revolution made the British monarchy into a constitutional one, subject through Parliament to the laws of the nation, although with no written constitution. Thus too the philosopher third Earl of Shaftesbury could write in 1712 of 'the spirit of the nation . . . grown more free'. When he sent his *Letter Concerning Design* to Lord Somers, Britain was still at war with Louis XIV of France. 'If we live,' wrote Shaftesbury, 'to see a peace any way answerable to that generous spirit with which this war was begun, and carried on, for our own liberty and that of Europe; the figure we are like to make abroad, and the increase of knowledge, industry and sense at home, will render united Britain the principal seat of arts: and by her politeness and advantages in this kind, will shew evidently, how much she owes to those counsels, which taught her to exert herself so resolutely on behalf of the common cause, and that of her own liberty, and happy constitution, necessarily included.'

Shaftesbury attacked the elderly Sir Christopher Wren and his works as representative of French taste and absolutism. Referring to hopes that were then still entertained, though never fulfilled, of a new royal palace in place of that burnt down in 1698, he wrote, 'Hardly, indeed, as the public now stands, should we bear to see a Whitehall treated like a Hampton Court, or even a new cathedral

Tunbridge Wells. The Pantiles. The pedestrian precinct was first laid out in 1638 in connection with the early spa.

like Saint Paul's. Almost everyone now becomes concerned, and interests himself in such public structures. Even those pieces too are brought under the common censure, which, though raised by private men, are of such a grandeur and magnificence, as to become national ornaments.'

'The people,' he continued, 'are no small parties in this cause. Nothing moves successfully without them. There can be no public, but where they are included. And without a public voice, knowingly guided and directed, there is nothing which can raise a true ambition in the artist; nothing which can exalt the genius of the workman, or make him emulous of after fame, and of the approbation of his country, and of posterity. For with these he naturally, as a free man, must take part: in these he has a passionate concern, and interest, raised in him by the same genius of liberty, the same laws and government, by which his property and the rewards of his pains and industry, are secured to him, and to his generation after him.'

In such a state, 'when the free spirit of a nation turns itself this way, judgements are formed, critics arise: the public eye and ear improve; a right taste prevails, and in a manner forces its way. Nothing is so improving, nothing so natural, so congenial to the liberal arts, as that reigning liberty and high spirit of a people . . . so much do we owe to the excellence of our national constitution, and legal monarchy.'

In this best of possible worlds, now that the problems of liberty, government and Scotland were solved, in 'united Britain the principal seat of arts', the progress of the arts and architecture 'knowingly guided and directed' would be assured. Shaftesbury was convalescing in Naples; his letter, sent to his noble friend in London and circulated in manuscript, predicted, among other things, but did not attempt to describe, a new national taste, a new British style in architecture. With the publication of the first volume of his *Vitruvius Britannicus* in 1715 the Scottish architect Colen Campbell nailed to the mast the colours of Inigo Jones (the British Vitruvius himself) and of Andrea Palladio, the chief architect of Renaissance Vicenza. After the latter the new style, which soon received the seal of noble taste and fashion from the young third Earl of Burlington, became known as Palladianism. Georgian architectural taste now had its prophets and, in Palladio's own book on architecture, its bible.

The Georgian city as a social ideal appeared to succeed, and did so for most of the eighteenth century. This was partly because during the course of the century there were some real social improvements, partly because distaste for the example of absolutist France was a strong incentive to ensure the success of an alternative social ideal, and partly because the 'people' wanted to believe in its success. To many of what are now seen to be its failings the 'people' turned a blind eye; indeed an obvious failing in modern eyes was the nature of the 'people'. Like the citizens of Ancient Athens they were those with a vote, for which they were qualified by a measure of substance and property; the unqualified masses had no more say than the Athenian slaves had had. The first extension of the franchise, and reforms of the often haphazard and corrupt parliamentary electoral system, were not to come until 1832; universal male suffrage was still far, and female suffrage even farther, in the future. Society favoured those who could keep their heads above water. Imprisonment for debt was commonplace and the outcome often hopeless. The spendthrift who lived on credit and never paid was not merely a stock character in stage comedies; most tradesmen were torn, and many were ruined, between giving credit with little hope of being paid and losing custom by refusing credit. In the building trades those who made contracts with the Crown knew that their accounts would, if slowly, eventually be settled.

The rural poor usually had enough to eat, although local or even national famine was always a possibility; there was a run of bad harvests in the 1760s and 70s. Their choice of food was limited but in the country it was wholesome and fresh. In towns real hunger was more common, and food was often adulterated or at the least stale. Improvements were made in hygiene, the supply of water, nutrition, agriculture and stock-breeding, and even in medicine; by 1800 the controversial practice of smallpox inoculation from a mild strain had been superseded by the safer method of vaccination with cowpox. Where industry grew the population grew through the influx of native workers, in search of employment, and of immigrants – Huguenots at the beginning of the eighteenth century and Irish at

Edinburgh. Royal High School, 1825–9. Thomas Hamilton.

the end, when the population of England, Wales and Scotland passed 10 million.

By then the steady increase in the birth rate and a fall in the death rate also contributed to the overcrowding of industrial towns, and the urban poor, underprivileged and unenfranchised, did not need intellectual reformers to stir up their discontents. Minor riots were frequent. The eighteenth century was an aggressive age; for much of it Britain was at war, though on foreign soil. The loss of the American colonies was not only a physical blow but also an emotional one, recalling to the country the filial alienation of the sons of its own kings. In the Napoleonic wars (1793–1815) there was a serious threat of a French invasion, and the increasing cost of war led to an economic slump in the 1790s. After 1815 there was a period of peace abroad but of increasing unrest at home in the industrial cities.

Cruelty and indifference took different forms from those of the twentieth century. Epidemic disease and early death were commonplace. Crowds went to watch the execution of criminals, and death was a punishment for many offences which would now be considered trivial. Other entertainments were the baiting of animals, cockfighting, and even observing the behaviour of lunatics in Bedlam. Gin

Dublin. Capel Street, looking towards Thomas Cooley's Royal Exchange, 1769–79.

was cheap, and squalid addiction to it was not uncommon. Women and small children worked long and arduous hours in mines and noisy mills for low wages, although this indicates not the heartlessness of employers but the absence of protective legislation and the necessity at almost any human price of an increase in family income. While bad employers treated their workers as chattels, good ones offered them a paternalism which nowadays seems to be acceptable only as the prerogative of cabinet ministers, trade-union leaders, planners and social workers. Governments accepted the doctrine of Adam Smith (1723–90) that private profit would bring public wealth, and that at home people should be left alone.

Established religion offered to human misfortune answers as dull and conventional as most eighteenth-century church buildings did to the eye. The eighteenth-century parson in the Church of England was better known for his table and his talk than for his sanctity or his social conscience. The unfortunate turned often to Wesleyan Methodism, in which emotions were not stifled by rationalism and human and divine truths were not smothered by worldly ambition. In Smollett's *Humphry Clinker* the amiable Squire Bramble found with consternation his womenfolk suddenly converted to Methodism by the eloquence of the title hero, who was of course his coachman

Brighton. Royal Pavilion, 1815–22. John Nash.

and, as it turned out, his own natural son. There were, too, true secular philanthropists who worked to improve the lot and the character of the ill-starred. Thomas Coram, a retired naval captain, established the Foundling Hospital in Bloomsbury in the 1740s to raise good sailors, servants and apprentices; he also projected an institution for the care of vagrants. Attempts at the reform of prisons were made by John Howard (1726–90), whose name is perpetuated in a society devoted to that end.

Against this background stood the extravagance, the conspicuous drinking and the gambling of a proportion of the wealthy; although the *New Bath Guide* (1766) is silent on the matter, the chief entertainment in Bath was gambling. Yet at the end of the period the ostentatious parties and the self-indulgence of George IV, who once told his father, 'However late I rise, the day is long enough for doing nothing', were both a disgrace and a magnificent side-show. The populace sided against him with Caroline of Brunswick, the earthy princess he officially married in 1795, slept with for one fruitful night but failed, because of the opposition of Parliament, to divorce. But George IV wearing the kilt was a great public success in Scotland and Ireland, and above all he was tolerated in society and forgiven in the retrospect of history because he had Taste.

Images of the Georgian City

Bath. The Circus, begun 1754. John Wood the Elder. Drawing by Thomas Malton, 1784.

The Rule of Taste

The model Georgian city, physically, is Bath. In 1813 all the developments of the previous ninety years there seemed to a French visitor to have been freshly cast at once in a single mould, and the remarkable homogeneity Bath still retains, in spite of modern depredation, is the result of several factors: its situation, its amenities, its personalities, the use of Bath stone, the skill and pride of the craftsmen, and the conventions of eighteenth-century design.

The situation of Bath on the north bank of a bend in the river Avon must have reminded the Romans of their mother city in the bend of the Tiber; the sunny south-facing slopes of Bath, first gentle and progressively steeper, form part of a natural basin in the hills which tempers the climate. To the Romans, the abundant and steaming mineral springs in the valley afforded not merely therapeutic facilities but also free hot water for a thermal complex like the much larger baths of Rome, in which body care was combined with the social amenities of a city club — recreation, urbane conversation and the transaction of business.

In the second quarter of the eighteenth century the remains of Roman Bath lay still unexcavated, but John Wood the Elder knew enough of its associations and its historical tradition to envisage a romantic evocation, not an archaeological resurrection, of the Ancient city for the successors of the Romans. It was at once less scholarly and more practical and liveable than Nicholas Hawksmoor's Baroque schemes of a decade earlier for Romanizing Oxford and Cambridge. By Wood's own account in his *Description of Bath* (2nd edn, 1749) it was in 1725–6 that he first proposed 'a grand Place of Assembly, to be called the Royal Forum . . . another Place . . . for the Exhibition of Sports, to be called the Grand Circus; and a third . . . for the Practice of medicinal Exercises, to be called the Imperial Gymnasium'. The North and South Parades, begun in 1740, are the only parts of the 'Forum' to be carried out, and the Gymnasium was a concept remote from eighteenth-century standards of recreation.

Bath. Air view of Great Pulteney Street and Laura Place, leading to Pulteney Bridge.

Ashby-de-la-Zouche. The Spa. Ivanhoe Baths, 1822. Robert Chaplin.

The Circus, begun in 1754, the year of his death, and completed by his son John Wood the Younger, shows clearly the unacademic essence of Wood's scholarship, for it was the first *modern* circus, circular in plan whereas the Roman ones, which were used for horse and chariot races, consisted of two long straights joined by semicircular ends. Wood actually had in mind not Roman circuses but oval amphitheatres like the Colosseum: Smollett recognized the Circus as 'like Vespasian's amphitheatre turned outside in'. Wood's transformation retains nothing of the prototype beyond the superimposed orders – he abandoned even the arcades of the Colosseum – but his artistic purpose was to soften the formality of the conventional urban shape, the square. The Circus was a masterpiece both pretty (Smollett's word) and, as will be seen later, influential.

The Circus was, of course, never used for sports; it is only a space, originally cobbled, surrounded by a terrace of thirty-three houses in three sections, with wedge-shaped party walls to make the interiors square. But it was the provision and development of proper amenities which allowed Bath to become and remain fashionable, and to grow in the course of the eighteenth century from a twice-yearly seasonal resort of the sick or idle wealthy for healing or gambling to a place with its own permanently resident society.

Medieval Bath shared a bishopric with Wells and was known for its textiles. The springs were rediscovered in the sixteenth century, and in the seventeenth the queens of James I, Charles II and James II all bathed there. The real fashion for Bath arose from the long stay of Queen Anne and Prince George, her consort, in 1702–3. Pre-Georgian Bath already possessed Assembly Rooms, a Pump Room, a Guildhall, an infirmary, and places to bathe and to walk about. Every spa had a pump room, every Georgian town except the smallest built its assembly rooms, though many were merely ballrooms added to inns; many towns (including Bath) acquired theatres. But although the proliferation of public buildings may not have been the cause of Bath's success as a place to live, the urban and social structures were certainly related.

Bath. Queen Square, 1729–36. View from the east side. John Wood the Elder. Drawing by Thomas Malton, 1784.

Liverpool. Town Hall. Built as the Exchange by John Wood the Elder in 1749–54.

Georgian Bath was indebted above all to three personalities. Richard 'Beau' Nash (1674–1762) was a professional gambler who in 1705 gained the post of Master of Ceremonies. Beau he was – Lord Chesterfield once mistook him for 'a gilt garland' – and Master he quickly became. Nash formulated rules of behaviour, which he upheld for the next thirty years with an authority attested by countless anecdotes. In 1715, 8,000 visitors came to Bath; during the season the totally idle life of 'Pump assemblies, walks, chocolate-houses, raffling-shops, medleys &c' described by Alexander Pope in the previous year needed as much organization as a present-day ocean cruise. While the chief entertainment was the craze of the time, gambling, and the next to it was scandal, Nash civilized the coarseness of the traditional aristocracy and formed the manners of the new rich. More than anyone he provided the ritual of Bath life.

Ralph Allen (1694–1764) arrived in Bath in 1715 as a post office clerk. Four years later he contracted to reform and develop for the Post Office the system of 'cross-posts' between towns on separate post roads, of which one has already been mentioned. Over a long period he progressively reduced frauds and increased his own revenue and that of the postal service. In 1742 he was Mayor of Bath. Meanwhile he had used his wife's dowry to buy and develop the quarries at Combe Down; this business venture gave Bath its beautiful texture, colour, and uniformity of material, and gave the name 'Bath stone' to a group of Somerset and Wiltshire oolite limestones, granular, good for dressing and carving, as various in colour as honey, and cheaper locally than brick.

John Wood (1704–54) was not the only speculative builder in early eighteenth-century Bath, but it was his romantic vision of a new Rome that utilized Allen's materials to fashion a noble setting for Nash's ritual, which would attract and hold the wealthy. But Wood, the son of a local builder, was no mere visionary. By the age of twenty-one when he produced his first scheme he was involved in building enterprises not only in his native Bath but in Yorkshire and on the Harley–Cavendish estate in the West End of London. In 1707 the Corporation of Bath had obtained the first of a number of Acts of Parliament empowering it to improve roads and provide lighting, cleansing and drainage for the streets; however, not all the

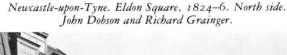

Newcastle-upon-Tyne. Eldon Square, 1824–6. North side.
John Dobson and Richard Grainger.

Bath. Lansdown Crescent, 1789–92. John Palmer.

city was in favour of building a new town, and in 1727 Wood's London financial backer, Robert Gay, curtailed his support for fear of political pressures. In May 1727 Wood settled permanently in Bath, and the following year he took the risky step of entering as sole contractor on the development of Queen Square, which he designed and built in 1729–36. Success rewarded his courage, and in the remainder of his somewhat short life he designed not only other domestic groups but the Assembly Rooms and the General Hospital in Bath, the Exchanges at Bristol and Liverpool, and Ralph Allen's country mansion, Prior Park, overlooking the city of Bath.

It is impossible to say what Bath would have been like if these three men had not come together in easy alliance; they were bound by their liking for the place, their business initiative and their success in identifying self-interest with the public good. What they saw in the steaming waters was gold. No committee hired them or investigated their profit motives, or could have remotely approached their achievement. Nor was their alliance unique in the Georgian period: at the end of it the commercial development of Newcastle-upon-Tyne was due to an architect, Dobson, a builder, Grainger, and the 'bland and prudent' town clerk John Clayton. In that instance Grainger lost an estimated £100,000 because he 'had a taste for art and was not bound to decorate his houses . . . but did it because it pleased him to do it'.

Wood also had 'a taste for art' and was no mean exponent of the English Palladian style in architecture. He must have learned building from his father, but his curious range of historical knowledge and fantasy suggests that in design he was self-taught. He found that previously 'the real use of the spade was unknown in, or about the City' and it was 'not till then, that the lever, the pulley, and the windlass, were introduced among the artificers' of the region. He diverted masons from Yorkshire and carpenters,

Bath. The Paragon, 1769–71. T. Warr Attwood. The high pavement separates the line of houses from the steep slope of the road.

joiners and plasterers from London and elsewhere: clearly the local building trades and crafts needed improvement, but the effects of Wood's raising of standards are to be found both in the visible parts and inside the carcase-work of Bath houses to the end of the Georgian era.

Before 1800 Bath was climbing up the hills: in 1791 Fanny Burney found the city greatly altered and its circumference tripled, though it is only fair to say that in 1816 she noted all year round 'the town at command' and 'the country for prospect, exercise and delight', whereas in 1766 Horace Walpole had found Bath detestably cramped. Nevertheless two of the virtues of Bath had been lost: compactness and exclusiveness. Mrs Delaney in 1736 had observed 'all the entertainments of the place in a small compass', a prerequisite of the tourist resort. The human scale of the buildings was to remain, but as the city grew, its golden ribbons winding up to Camden Crescent and Lansdown Crescent, the loss of advantages of neo-Republican social amenities within an easy walk could for higher dwellers only be balanced by the fresher air, sunshine and scenic views over the city to the southern hills.

This change of attraction contributed to Bath's endurance. Smollett about 1770 not only observed that the inflated cost of living there was driving the poorer gentility to cheaper and deeply provincial places like Exeter, effectively more remote than York, he also contrasted Bath's stable growth with the instability of other spas. Scarborough no longer had any distinction, and Sheridan's *Journey to Scarborough* could as well have been set anywhere else. Vanbrugh's nephew Edward, who had a house in Brock Street, near the Circus, wrote in 1773 that 'fresh people pour in upon us every day . . . evening amusements are . . . thick upon the back of another'. But the Royal Family went to Cheltenham in 1788; in the same decade the fifth Duke of Devonshire began to develop Buxton as a spa to compete with Bath, and George III and the Prince of Wales acquired a taste, at Weymouth and Brighton, for the newer fashion of sea bathing.

Smollett's Squire Bramble found Bath the centre of 'racket and dissipation', the Circus too far from the public buildings and its access through Gay Street 'difficult, steep, and slippery'. He went

Bath. Royal Crescent, 1767–74. John Wood the Younger.

on: 'the rage of building has laid hold on such a number of adventurers, that one sees new houses starting up in every out-let and every corner of Bath; contrived without judgement, executed without solidity, and stuck together . . . like the wreck of streets and squares disjointed by an earthquake, which hath broken the ground into a variety of holes and hillocks . . . What sort of a monster Bath will become in a few years, with these growing excrescences, may be easily conceived.' This is the view of rheumatic middle age as the gradients increased, although while the 1790s saw improvements to the old town centre the combination of over-building and the war with France led to a slump until after 1815. Smollett offers the contrasting conventional view of the squire's niece, that 'The Square, the Circus, and the Parades put you in mind of the sumptuous palaces represented in prints and pictures; and the new buildings . . . look like so many enchanted castles,

Lancaster. Nos. 5–7 Queen Street. One of many ingenious and unconventional uses of paired doorways to link two terrace houses.

raised on hanging terraces.' It is certain that, while much of Bath may still seem to be the product of magic, it was not the product of any overall plan.

The relation of regularity to freedom will be discussed in the following sections; first the remaining factor in the making of the city must be considered: the conventions of design, or, in the elusive term of the period, Taste. Taste was, like Charity, the greatest and the essential virtue. Without it no effort was of avail; in its name every excess or failure of judgement could be excused. It was valued rather by critics and patrons than by artists, for whereas imagination precedes the artistic process, Taste is only apparent in the completed work. Its fascination as an ideal derived from the combination of three different ideas, decorum, conformity and tradition.

Decorum was a seventeenth-century criterion, of what was appropriate in either the choice and representation of subjects in art or the treatment of formal values; it was moral and aesthetic. Conformity on the other hand was a social, or even a political, criterion: the consensus of opinion among the enlightened, which Shaftesbury had expected would produce a new art and architecture.

Historians long ago recognized that in politics Shaftesbury's ordered, elegant, uniform Britain existed only as an ideal; they have been much less inclined to make the parallel with the arts of the time, and clichés of elegance, grace and an innate sense of proportion still abound in historical writing. The Augustans believed in order and in systems of order, and if they imagined both the universe and the state to tick like a clockwork machine it was entirely reasonable to expect the creative mind to follow golden rules of similar predictability. Combining decorum and conformity would seem bound to lead shortly to a canon of timid mediocrity. In fact, Georgian design is seldom exciting, but it generally excels, not because it is decorous or conformist, or because it is Georgian, or rational, but because it is in a long tradition of excellence.

Rising affluence in the growing middle classes offered plenty of work to a large number of craftsmen who were proud of their skills, worked in the best materials and — provided they were paid — earned a good livelihood. The desire of each level of society to ape the one above it made the pursuit of gentility a moral virtue and helped to raise and maintain standards of design. But as long as things were made by hand the only thing new about the designers' methods was the increasing range and availability of patterns in engravings in addition to those made and kept by individuals and handed on from master to pupil. The architect, the painter and the craftsman scaled and proportioned their works according to their purpose and according to rules of thumb which, like recipes for materials and techniques, had been handed down from the Middle Ages. For centuries the Golden Mean, for example, has been considered a dimensional ratio of peculiar efficacy, but demonstrations of its use in practical rather than theoretical cases are often self-deceiving:

believing in it was more important than relying upon it.

While decorative details vary with date and materials with locality, one Georgian street front is much like another. The *Four Books of Architecture* of Palladio, first published in Venice in 1570 and first issued in English translation by Giacomo Leoni in 1716–20, was the most important book for Georgian architecture not only because Palladianism became the name of the Inigo Jones revival, but because it suggested that architectural design could be reduced to a series of formulas. This was an aesthetic concept, but it became inseparable from a utilitarian one. The Great Fire of 1666 had put an end to wooden house building in London, and a series of smaller disasters in provincial towns over the following 100 years showed that timber was no longer a suitable urban building material. Between 1670 and 1774 successive Acts of Parliament laid down

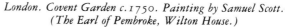

London. Covent Garden c.1750. Painting by Samuel Scott.
(The Earl of Pembroke, Wilton House.)

progressively tighter standards for the construction, and especially the façades, of London street houses, determining the heights of storeys, the size and setting in of windows and the minimum width of streets of various classes, and restricting the use of wood even in the making of windows. These Acts had no force in the provinces beyond that of good example, but one of Wood's importations into Bath was undoubtedly the London standards of construction. Of almost equal significance was to be his introduction there of the London square.

The London Square

The first London square was Covent Garden, designed by Inigo Jones and built in 1631–5 for the fourth Earl of Bedford. Several of its features were unusual but were to be momentous for the future. The scheme was the product of a bargain between the Earl, who

Buxton. The Crescent, begun c.1780. John Carr of York.

wanted to make money from his land, and the Crown, which charged him £2,000 for a licence to build in an area subject to a ban on new building. By special pleading the ban was circumvented by classing the work as redevelopment, and Jones, the King's Surveyor, was given overall control. The house interiors could be planned as individual leaseholders wished, so long as the fronts were uniform. The scheme included on the west side a church, while the centres of the north and east sides were taken by streets extending the new orderliness beyond the confines of the square.

The whole area was indubitably improved, and the church helped to make it a neighbourhood centre. The precedents were recent and monumental: Jones knew both the cathedral and *piazza* laid out at Leghorn by Ferdinando de' Medici and the Place Royale in Paris laid out by Henri IV of France. Of Covent Garden's two other features one was individual, the other became essential to the Georgian city. The individual feature was the ground floor arcades, modelled on the foreign sources, and rarely repeated in Britain, although Carr of

York's Crescent at Buxton (*c*.1780) is a fine exception. The other feature was on the south side, where the new square and the back garden of Bedford House were seen to be extensions of one another. The residents had the attraction of a desirable locality, and the Earl had a view, open in the middle ground and closed by the most modern buildings in Westminster.

This feature recurs in the first square to be so called, Southampton (now Bloomsbury) Square, which was begun by the Earl of Southampton in 1661 in front of his house and became the nucleus of Georgian Bloomsbury. The diarist John Evelyn referred to 'a whole Square or Piazza & little Towne', and the residents had the advantages not only of proximity to the Earl but also of their own market in one of the subsidiary streets laid out from the square. Lord Southampton introduced the system of building leases, which became general for town house building: individuals could build houses for subleasing, or have them built for their own occupation, on payment of a ground rent for the use of the site. When the lease expired the property reverted to the owner of the ground and could be re-leased. The return for the ground landlord was slow, steady, and permanent; the speculative builder's outlay was considerable

London. Hanover Square, 1787. In the distance is St George's Church, 1720–5, by John James.

Bath. Queen Square, 1729–36. North side. John Wood the Elder. The original sash windows with glazing bars and small panes have been replaced by Victorian plate windows.

but the quick return he expected on his houses was his incentive to complete them.

The market places in the centre of British towns changed little between the Middle Ages and the middle of the twentieth century. Many of them are small and irregular in shape, though there are large rectangular ones at, for instance, King's Lynn in Norfolk and Masham in Yorkshire. Nothing is more dead than an English market place when the shops have closed. The French *place* and Italian *piazza*, on the other hand, never quite go to sleep, and continental Europeans in general live in the street far more than the British. The word 'square', which the French have appropriated, implies a rectangular space, but English has no other equivalent for *piazza*: Saint Peter's Square in Rome is of course oval, and at Covent Garden the arcades came to be known as 'the piazzas'. Such spaces in European cities are centres of public activity and have hard edges between buildings and pavement. In Georgian streets and squares edges were softened by the introduction of areas, open to cellar level in front of all but the humblest houses, fenced with an iron railing and separating the house front from a coal store that extended out beneath the pavement.

The centre of the London square was more private than public space. Even where it was not laid out as a garden for the residents, it had the character of a courtyard or a college quadrangle rather than a thoroughfare, a species of open interior rather than an assemblage of exteriors, and a space more to be looked at through house windows than to be used. The gradual introduction of grass and trees in the middle of squares blurred further the division between building and nature and established the suburban nature of the Georgian city. It can hardly be accidental that the country house in its landscape park was the other great manifestation of Georgian architectural endeavour.

The architecture of squares did not always give the impression of a great open room. St James's Square was planned by Lord St Albans in the 1660s to include his own house, but there was little uniformity in the façades. Bristol's Queen Square, commemorating Queen Anne's visit in 1702, was generally although not rigorously uniform, but so large as to resemble four separate streets; the same is true sixty years later of the regular and even larger Merrion Square in Dublin. By the 1720s, however, there were experiments in tying together a whole terrace of individual houses as if they were one palace front, having a central pavilion with a pediment and applied portico, and often end pavilions as well. The north and east sides of Grosvenor Square were designed in this way, though Edward Shepherd who built the north side failed to acquire the whole block and could not align his centrepiece with the middle of the square. John Wood, who knew Shepherd, applied the idea more successfully to the north side of Queen Square, Bath, though his programme of palace fronts there was not completed. From then on uniformity became the general practice, although as late as the 1770s some large squares like Portman Square in St Marylebone were designed piecemeal. In Cavendish Square, on the other hand, the two ends of the north side, built by Shepherd about 1720, became fifty years later the setting for the two freestanding mansions that still form the centrepiece. Some of the finest later Georgian street architecture is to be found in square fronts, including Robert Adam's in Charlotte Square, Edinburgh, and Fitzroy Square, London, Gillespie Graham's Hamilton Square, Birkenhead, and Bedford Square, London (possibly by Thomas Leverton).

All these examples started or ended as the kernels of larger grids

Edinburgh. Charlotte Square, begun 1791. North side. Robert Adam.

of new streets, to which they stood in the same relation of rank as the mansions held to the earliest squares. In Bath and the West End of London the rate and scale of new building increased, and elsewhere New Towns were planned on rectangular grids. These schemes were of two kinds, utilitarian new towns as planned communities, and new middle- and upper-class suburbs to existing towns. In both kinds new land was staked out in conditions not unlike those in the American colonies.

In Ireland, in the course of English colonization, small towns had

been created since the early seventeenth century on grid plans, in contrast to the traditional Irish pattern of a single long and often very broad street. In Britain too there were a few totally new planned towns related to new industries. Whitehaven was begun in the 1680s to import tobacco; later, like Maryport (begun in 1748, also in Cumbria) it was an outlet for the local coalmining industry. Ardrossan (Ayrshire) was begun in 1806 as the sea port for a canal to Paisley and Glasgow, and, like the canal scheme, never completed. New regular small towns were built at Fochabers, Morayshire (from 1776), to be further away from Gordon Castle, and at Cullen, Banffshire (from 1822), where the Earl of Seafield considered it more economic than perpetually repairing the old town. Much as in seventeenth-century European towns of these types, and in New England examples such as New Haven, Connecticut, the square at the heart of the grid owed nothing to London: it was public and corporate, a meeting- or market-place bordered by church and civic buildings.

Small-scale improvements were more often in the form of single

Fairfield near Manchester. Moravian Settlement, begun 1785.

*Birmingham. The Crescent, begun 1795 and abandoned.
John Rawsthorne and Charles Norton.*

streets. Castle Street, Bridgwater, was laid out for the Duke of Chandos in 1721 in connection with his investment in local industrial schemes for distilling and soap- and glass-making. There were also small inland waterside developments like the Avon Quay at Bath and the individual houses of North Brink and South Brink on the Nene in the middle of Wisbech. Seventy years later, at the top of Bridgnorth, East Castle Street was planned with a new church at the end. A new square round a new church was not uncommon: those of St John's, Wolverhampton, and St Paul's, Birmingham, about 1770, were originally handsome. In Westminster, St John, Smith Square, and St George, Hanover Square (actually outside the square), had been financed by the 1711 Act of Parliament for new churches in the metropolis.

Mention should also be made of the Settlements planned and built by the Moravians, a Protestant sect, in the middle of the eighteenth century, such as Fairfield near Manchester. The sense of calm and order of these 'model villages' has a religious and utilitarian basis different from the political foundations of the Georgian City.

Edinburgh. George Square, 1766–85. Built by James Brown and named after his brother.

The later Georgian high-class 'New Town' suburbs include after 1800 the 'West End' (actually to the east) of Liverpool and in London the Bloomsbury (Bedford) and Belgravia (Grosvenor) estates, but the first comprehensive large projects were the product of Scottish initiative and engineering.

Edinburgh's cultural revival, and the collapse of a block in the High Street, gave the impetus in 1752 to break from the confines of the old city: first south to George Square about 1760, and then, by bridging the volcanic ravine of the North Loch, to a spacious new area on the north, half a mile long with squares at each end, a grid of streets, with provision for churches and public buildings, including a Merchants' Exchange and a repository for national records. The design of this grid, entrusted in 1766 to James Craig, provided only for general uniformity. Adam's Charlotte Square block of 1791 was thus quite new for Edinburgh in aesthetic quality, but gave the following builders precedents for regularity and the use of the classical orders. When William Laird the Scots shipbuilder laid out a grid at Birkenhead, twice the size of Craig's New Town, his architect was Gillespie Graham of Edinburgh; Grainger of Newcastle also acknowledged the influence of Edinburgh.

A New Town begun in Aberdeen in 1799 was unsuccessful; a more modest scheme in Perth joined the two parallel streets of the old town with a grid. In Glasgow regular streets were laid out in increasing numbers after about 1750, but building houses on them was slow. St Andrew's Square, begun 1768, was the first of several squares around churches or public buildings. The large, well-articulated George Square was begun in 1787. 1802 saw the commencement of the palace terraces of Carlton Place south of the Clyde. Several New Town suburbs followed, and Glasgow architecture continued to be 'Georgian' in style until after 1850.

Scottish enterprise also produced one great work of architecture and engineering in London, the vaults and terraces of the Adelphi built by the Adam brothers between the Strand and the Thames between 1768 and 1772. As engineering it was sound, as scenery it was commanding; as a speculation it failed and did the Adams lasting harm. As architecture its reputation has perhaps been inflated since its destruction to make way for Shell-Mex House.

Nature and Artifice

One of the least-assimilated lessons of modern planning is how scale affects mistakes: small-scale errors can be valuable and fertile, whereas in large plans they are not only nearly inevitable but also disastrous. Any city extended beyond human scale creates human conflicts, but a grid does not have to extend very far for feelings of oppression to overtake those of order and reassurance. By the 1760s the imaginations of developers and their architects were influenced by the ideas that produced the landscape garden, in which nature's accidents and irregularities were adapted and improved or, where they were lacking, supplied by artifice.

Bath, not London, led the way, in the Woods' imaginative use of sites. Queen Square slopes a little, and Gay Street rises from one corner of it to the Circus. The latter has three approach streets, and

Brock Street and its surroundings to the west are thus out of square to the Gay Street area. This much was the elder Wood's conception, and we do not know whether it was father or son who conceived the extension of Brock Street into one end of the Royal Crescent, begun

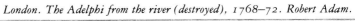

London. The Adelphi from the river (destroyed), 1768–72. Robert Adam.

in 1767. The Crescent is half a Colosseum in plan though not in elevation; that is, half an oval. This produced two innovations. First, the sloping ground gave the houses their own landscaped park; second, every house in the Crescent gives a pleasing view not of its close but of its remoter neighbours, so that the street architecture itself becomes part of the scenic setting of each house.

Bath. Air view of Royal Crescent and the Circus. In the distance are Lansdown Crescent on the left and Camden Place on the right.

Squire Bramble predicted after the Crescent a Star and, by 1800 perhaps, 'all the signs of the Zodiac exhibited in architecture at Bath'. Actuality was more regular, but new shapes and landscaping became popular. 'The form of a crescent always takes', wrote Jane Austen, and by 1800 this shape was a cliché. Crescents were built to command views: on hills at Bath, in the new seaside resorts of the south coast, even in town centres (Buxton, Cheltenham), though the builder of Birmingham's went bankrupt after a few houses because the area was out of fashion. Nash's colonnaded Park Crescent serves to funnel Regent's Park into Portland Place, the rural into the urban terraces. Curvatures varied; the red brick Crescent at Taunton is nearly straight. Cornwallis Crescent, Clifton (1791), overlooks gardens and has its street behind on the convex side, while Clifton's Paragon is set in the reverse sense. 'Paragon' is not a geometrical shape but a 'model of its kind'; however, straight and curved Paragons became fashionable, as well as Polygons, Ovals, and Circuses. Bedford Circus, Exeter, was an elegant long oval; the famous Oval at Kennington remained largely undeveloped.

The West End of Edinburgh has several long ovals made of two facing and separately named crescents. Nearby Melville Street is divided in the middle by a lozenge-shaped place very like Laura Place in Great Pulteney Street at Bath. There are also a round Royal Circus and the basically hexagonal Moray Place, one of whose exits leads through the oval Ainslie Place to the middle of Randolph Crescent. But in spite of these varied and linked shapes the Edinburgh New Towns retain a rather grim, and, by contrast with either Bath stone or Nash's London stucco, a grey correctness. New Edinburgh's high point, literally, is Calton Hill to the east where, except for the long Royal Terrace, buildings were placed according to the lie of the landscape to form the Acropolis of *Modern Athens*. The finest and most original building is Thomas Hamilton's Royal

Bristol. Clifton. The Paragon, 1809–14. Built by John Drew.
Concave side, facing the street.

Cheltenham. Pittville Pump Room, 1825–30. John Forbes.

High School (1825–9), impeccable in neo-Greek purity of line, mass and detailing. The Athenian reference, stressed by the monument to Dugald Stewart in the form of that of Lysicrates in Athens, would have been complete if the National Monument, to the Napoleonic War, had not been abandoned for lack of funds: it was to have been a replica of the Parthenon.

Calton Hill's mixture of landscape, learning and national pride is unique in Britain, although a similar mixture is to be found in several European capitals, most notably the Munich of Ludwig I of Bavaria. Moreover, as early as the 1760s Giovanni Battista Piranesi's engraved restoration of the ancient Campus Martius in Rome and Adam's plates of Diocletian's Palace at Split had offered a new theoretical basis for obliqueness and informality on an imperial scale. Munich too has its English Garden, an urban landscape park which, size apart, strikes the English as ordinarily municipal, but which belongs to the same process of expansion and loosening of urban structure that in Britain runs from Royal Crescent at Bath to Regent's Park and to Cheltenham.

Cheltenham's rise from a small market town with a cold mineral spring began modestly about 1740 as an economical rustic alternative to sophisticated Bath. The Act of Parliament of 1786 for street paving was perhaps not unconnected with the suggestion two years later that George III should come to drink the waters. By 1792 canal works made building stone accessible, and the discovery of several more mineral wells encouraged the simultaneous development of Pittville north and Lansdown south of the town. The Peace of 1815 brought a boom until about 1840 when Continental spas became more popular, and Cheltenham became famous for schools. In comparison with Bath, Cheltenham was almost flat. The replacement of any pattern of grids and squares by a series of crescents and sometimes deliberately serpentine streets is thus a considered attempt to make the natural landscape more interesting visually. Moreover, from the 1820s onwards formal terraces were mixed with single or paired residences known as 'villas' on the model of Nash's Park Villages in Regent's Park.

In 1811, as the British economy began to recover towards the close of the Napoleonic War, two things happened. Prince George was made Regent, and the lease of Marylebone Park reverted to the Crown. The scheme devised by John Fordyce, Surveyor of Land Revenue, and John Nash, architect, courtier, and intimate of the Prince, was for a vast landscape garden containing lakes, canals, individual villas, picturesque villages, and huge terraces. To attract the noble and high-class office-holders of Whitehall and Westminster, Regent's Park was to connect with Portland Place and a new street running south to Carlton House overlooking St James's

Park. After 1820, when most of Regent Street had been built, the Regent became George IV and moved to Buckingham Palace. Carlton House was replaced by a Nash terrace named after it. The provision of housing in the park was almost entirely limited in the end to the Park Villages and one large ring of terraces built in the 1820s round the edge, and the scheme was not without financial troubles. Nevertheless, in this modified form it was finished.

London. Regent's Park. Cumberland Terrace, 1821–30. John Nash and James Thomson.

Nothing has remained of Nash's Regent Street since the 1920s except its line, including Piccadilly and Oxford Circuses and the Quadrant, and the church of All Souls, Langham Place, whose spike-steeple marks the point where Upper Regent Street sidesteps into Portland Place. The street's erratic course was designed to avoid or incorporate obstacles, but it is in his sense of the scenic rather than in the use of stucco that Nash's real mastery lies. After damage in the Second World War and years of uncertainty the terrace fronts have now been restored and the house interiors modernized for a new lease of life.

Buildings and People

Georgian sea-bathing was an extension of spa-bathing. It was popularized in the 1750s by Dr Richard Russell of Brighton, who controlled the local spring. The sea was not friendly, and for non-swimmers sudden total immersion by a hired baptist was traumatic.

Brighton. Adelaide Crescent, Hove, begun 1830. Decimus Burton.

Brighton. Royal Crescent, 1798–1807. Built by J. B. Otto. The houses are faced with black mathematical tiles.

The patronage of the Prince of Wales from 1783, and the proximity of a huge military camp from 1793, made Brighton popular, but the resort developed with its back to the sea; even the Royal Pavilion, which grew from a modest villa to become by 1820 a vast Kubla Khan palace, lies back and faces landward. But by 1835 the seafront, from Kemp Town on the east to Hove on the west, extended for a mile and a half in a string of three- and four-storey crescents, parades, terraces and squares. The offshore impression of a vast city was illusory, for Brighton was still only a marine Regent's Park, one block deep, the ideal of the modern resort with a sea-view from every room.

Before 1837 the sea-craze and its architecture extended sporadically from Weymouth to Margate, but admiring the sea as a landscape unmoulded by Man was a Romantic idea, new in itself and no less so for a seafaring nation that traditionally considered Neptune a divinity to be fought with, vanquished and exploited. Georgian Britain produced no seaport city on the scale of Copen-

Newcastle-upon-Tyne. Royal Arcade (demolished), 1831–2. John Dobson and Richard Grainger.

hagen, St Petersburg or Helsinki, where ocean sailing ships moored across the square from the seat of government.

London entered the Georgian period with Wren's new cathedral so hedged about that its lower part could only be viewed obliquely. The broad quays planned after the Great Fire were never built, and modern London has no continuous embankment roadway. A model of what might have been is viceregal Dublin in colonial Ireland: Dublin's imposing domed public buildings, Custom House, Courts, King's Inns, Exchange and the Irish Parliament (which was run from Westminster) were more truly imperial emblems than all Nash's London terraces. Bristol, the largest port besides London from the Middle Ages, had a Georgian dockland centre; the half square mile between the two arms of the Floating Harbour retains Queen Square, the Exchange and Theatre Royal and many individual large merchants' houses.

In Liverpool, which came to supplant Bristol, the wide Mersey waterfront has since changed dramatically, but the original dock of 1709–21 was in the old town at the end of Castle Street; when the basin was filled to make Canning Place, John Foster's domed Custom House was built there (1828–39). Halfway up Castle Street stood St George's church (the first 1720, the second 1825 by Foster). These buildings have gone, but John Wood's Exchange at the other end of Castle Street survives as the Town Hall (or rather Mansion House) with a dome and portico added by the Elder Foster after a fire in 1795.

In Newcastle a different kind of development took place. The city bordered on the precipitous slopes of the Tyne valley; by 1830 the filling in of many of the rifts in the valley had much improved the streets and layout of the city. Newcastle was prosperous enough to have a purpose-built commercial centre around Grey and Grainger Streets, designed and managed by John Dobson and Richard Grainger, with stone-built façades more distinguished than Nash's Regent Street.

Newcastle's Royal Arcade (1831–2, destroyed) gave covered access to shops, a news room, auction rooms, and baths, with vaulted offices underground. However, the separation of pedestrians was not new. It was to be found in spas, for example the famous

Leamington Spa. The Parade, c.1815–33. In the distance is Christ Church, 1825, by P. F. Robinson.

Pantiles at Tunbridge Wells. The New Walk at Leicester was laid out as a suburban promenade in 1785 and, though built around, remains a broad walk.

Growth in both population and affluence meant more people with common interests and urban pleasures. Besides theatres and assemblies for dancing there were now buildings for cultural societies, exhibitions, tableaux, panoramas, and suburban pleasure gardens. London's early Georgian Vauxhall acquired a rival at Ranelagh, and in 1750 there were Vauxhalls in Bristol and Birmingham. The theatre took hold even in Calvinist Edinburgh. While local government was rudimentary, the public well-being required new and larger shire, town and market halls and law courts; industry required banks and offices. Monuments were not very common. Among others an obelisk of 1788 at Kendal to Liberty commemorates 1688. The first column to Nelson (1817) is at Yarmouth. A statue of George III at Weymouth thanks him for his patronage, and an obelisk at Ramsgate thanks George IV for travelling that way on his visit to Hanover in 1820.

The stirrings of social conscience, or the fear of ignorance, civil disorder or epidemic, led to an increase in colleges, libraries, asylums, gaols and hospitals. New suburbs needed places of worship for both the Established and nonconformist churches. Better roads meant more traffic and better bridges: many late Georgian bridges survive, reinforced, after two centuries. The purpose of buildings did not yet greatly affect their exterior style, only their shape. Before about 1780 most new churches and public buildings alike were Palladian. In the next half-century Athens replaced Rome: most secular buildings and some churches were neo-Greek. But churches were increasingly neo-Gothic, and in 1836 the new Houses of Parliament design set a general seal of approval on medievalism. At Leamington, which was a small village in 1800 but grew meteorically after 1815 in competition with Cheltenham as a spa, the Parade was aligned on a neo-Norman church (now destroyed).

The creation of the Georgian City spanned more than a century. If we now need imagination to re-create its perfection, its original inhabitants needed determination and optimism ever to realize it. Thomas Malton's views about 1790 show that perfection best, but in many places it was not quickly achieved. One after another, individual city and parish councils obtained private Acts of Parliament authorizing them to levy rates on property for paving, lighting (by oil lamps), draining, cleansing and patrolling the new streets. In the 1750s St Marylebone was favourably compared in these respects with Westminster; the City of Canterbury had no such general facilities before 1787. The supply of water, by private companies, also varied from place to place. In parts of London they competed, their main supply pipes criss-crossing under the new pavements. Leaks were common, and the workmen who came to repair them could be relied upon to replace the damaged paving with gravel!

We must also hear the noise of hooves, iron wheels and street cries. It was usual to meet sheep, cattle and geese being driven live to market, and Marylebone Road was built to keep them out of the new residential areas. Everyday goods were sold in local markets or

[63]

London. Lower Regent Street, looking south from Piccadilly Circus to Carlton House and Westminster Hall. Lithograph from a drawing by T. H. Shepherd, 1822.

by travelling vendors. There were carts and carriages of every shape, size and speed, and in some areas horse-dung was so abundant that market gardeners would not buy it. The greatest traffic danger to pedestrians was the sedan chair: the chairmen went at the double, with the inertia of two strong bodies plus the chair and passenger, with limited powers of steering and none of stopping.

The structure of Georgian society has disappeared for ever. Artefacts outlive actions, and some of the fabric of Georgian cities survives. Conserving the best is our duty both to our forebears' vision and to our posterity's expectation. Stone does not last for ever, but neither consolidating nor replacing it, neither painting woodwork nor banning motor vehicles, can do more than provide a framework for acts of the imagination. Architecture gives order, dignity and visual enhancement to human activities. When the life-style which elicited particular architectural solutions passes, the aesthetic qualities remain; thus it may be pleasurable and uplifting still to work in a Georgian room or walk in a Georgian square.